Using Primary Sources
to Meet Common Core State Standards

Authors: Schyrlet Cameron and Suzanne Myers

Editors: Mary Dieterich and Sarah M. Anderson

Proofreader: Margaret Brown

COPYRIGHT © 2014 Mark Twain Media, Inc.

ISBN 978-1-62223-461-5

Printing No. CD-404212

Mark Twain Media, Inc., Publishers
Distributed by Carson-Dellosa Publishing LLC

Table of Contents

To the Teacher

In the past, middle-school students viewed history through the eyes of their textbook and other secondary sources. Giving students access to primary sources allows them to become historians. Through the process of examining, analyzing, and interpreting historical documents, students become engaged in inquiry-based learning. This leads them to a deeper understanding of historical events.

Using Primary Sources covers a variety of historical events. This book is designed to offer teachers a wide range of instructional options to meet the diverse learning styles of middle-school students. The activities can be used for independent practice and small-group or classroom instruction. This book is divided into three sections.

Instructional Resources can be used as teacher-directed introductory lessons. They are designed to show students how to identify primary and secondary sources, evaluate primary sources, and recognize fact and opinion.

Document-Based Learning Activities provide students with opportunities to work with primary and secondary sources. For most activities, facsimiles and transcriptions of primary and secondary sources have been included in the book. All efforts have been made to maintain the formatting, capitalization, punctuation, and spelling as found in the original documents. A few documents must be accessed online. For these documents, the URL has been provided. This section is divided into three parts.

- **Single Source:** Individual primary source documents are followed by a page of document-based questions or activities.

- **Multi-Text Sources:** Two primary sources on a single topic are followed by document-based questions.

- **Text With Audio/Visual Source:** Primary and secondary documents in print format are integrated with primary sources in visual or auditory format. They are followed by document-based questions.

    The learning activities require students to support their answers with details or evidence. The questions cover reading comprehension skills, such as locating information, determining the meaning of words or phrases, identifying point of view, drawing inferences, and citing evidence.

The Learning Stations Activity requires students to examine, analyze, and interpret primary and secondary sources focusing on Abraham Lincoln and the character traits that made him an effective leader during the Civil War.

The Common Core State Standards for English Language Arts include standards for Literacy in History/Social Studies. The activities in this book can be taught within the English Language Arts content area or can be used as interdisciplinary units between English Language Arts and History/Social Studies.

Common Core State Standards Matrix

English Language Arts Standards: Literacy in History/Social Studies

Units of Study	RH.6-8.1	RH.6-8.2	RH.6-8.3	RH.6-8.4	RH.6-8.5	RH.6-8.6	RH.6-8.7	RH.6-8.8	RH.6-8.9	RH.6-8.10
Instructional Resources								X		X
Document-Based Learning Activities: Single Source	X	X		X		X				X
Document-Based Learning Activities: Multi-Text Sources	X	X				X		X		X
Document-Based Learning Activities: Text With Audio/Visual Sources	X	X				X	X		X	X
Learning Station Activities: American Civil War: Characteristics of a Leader	X	X		X		X	X	X	X	X

Types of Primary Sources

A **primary source** is a firsthand account or physical object that was written or created during the time period being studied. Primary sources make it possible for you to become historians by interpreting historical events for yourself.

advertisements	furniture	poetry
audio recordings	interviews	political cartoons
autobiographies	jewelry	postcards
autographs	journals	posters
award certificates	land records	report cards
bank records	legal documents	sales receipts
baseball cards	legislation	school transcripts
birth certificates	letters	scrapbooks
blueprints	magazines	sheet music
brochures	manuscripts	sketchbooks
bus schedules	maps	song lyrics
census records	marriage licenses	speeches
clothing	medals	stamps
coins	membership cards	tax records
contracts	memoirs	team statistics
court records	menus	telegrams
death certificates	military records	tombstones
deeds	newsletters	tools
diaries	newspapers	toys and games
diplomas	oral histories	trophies
drawings	paintings	video recordings
driver's licenses	patents	wills
e-mails	photographs	yearbooks

Types of Secondary Sources

A **secondary source** is a secondhand account or physical object that was created by someone using information from primary sources or other secondary sources.

almanacs	dictionaries	handbooks
atlases	directories	history books
biographies	encyclopedias	manuals
chronologies	guidebooks	textbooks

Evaluating a Primary Source

Every primary source may not be credible or reliable. Whoever created the source may have had a **bias** or slanted perspective of the event. For example, if you are reading a firsthand account of the Battle of Gettysburg written by a Union soldier, you must realize that the account of the battle, while factual, may be biased. Bias is one reason that it is important to evaluate every primary source. Ask yourself the following questions when evaluating a primary source.

Author/Creator
- Who created the source?
- What was the person's role in the event: participant or eyewitness?
- When and where was the source created?

Audience/Purpose
- Who was the intended audience?
- Why was the source created: to inform, persuade, entertain, or describe?
- Does the purpose affect the reliability of the source?

Content/Reliability
- What type of source is it?
- What kind of information does the source contain?
- Can the information be supported by other sources?

Point of View/Bias
- What is the person's point of view or perspective?
- Does the content seem objective, or can you detect bias?
- Is there evidence to support the person's claims?

Name: _____   Date: _____

Primary Source Evaluation Form

1. Title of the primary source: _____

2. Type of primary source: _____

3. **Author/Creator:** Who created the source? What was the person's role in the event: participant or eyewitness? When and where was the source created?

   _____

   _____

   _____

   _____

4. **Audience/Purpose:** Who was the intended audience? Why was the source created? Does the purpose affect the reliability of the source?

   _____

   _____

   _____

   _____

5. **Content/Reliability:** What kind of information does the source contain? Can the information be supported by other sources?

   _____

   _____

   _____

   _____

6. **Point of View/Bias:** What is the person's point of view or perspective? Does the content seem objective, or can you detect bias? Is there evidence to support the person's claims?

   _____

   _____

   _____

   _____

Name: _____ Date: _____

Recognizing Fact and Opinion

It is important to evaluate every primary source. In order to evaluate a primary source, you need to be able to recognize the difference between fact and opinion. A **fact** is something that can be proven true with some form of evidence. An **opinion** expresses what a person or group thinks, feels, or believes. Opinion statements may contain signal words or phrases such as *best, most, probably, I believe, I think,* or *I feel.*

Directions: Read each statement below. Place the letter **F** on the line if the statement is a fact. Place the letter **O** on the line if the statement is an opinion.

_____ 1. Abraham Lincoln was the sixteenth President of the United States.

_____ 2. The transcontinental railroad was completed on May 10, 1869.

_____ 3. I think Christopher Columbus was the greatest explorer in history.

_____ 4. Settlers of the Great Plains were called sodbusters.

_____ 5. George Washington was probably the most intelligent general of the American Revolution.

George Washington

_____ 6. The Mayflower Compact gave Pilgrims the right to govern themselves.

_____ 7. Patrick Henry's speeches were more persuasive than the speeches of Daniel Webster.

_____ 8. The cotton gin was the most important invention of the Industrial Revolution.

_____ 9. In my opinion, the Spanish Armada was the greatest naval force in history.

_____ 10. The French and Indian War was one of the events that led to the American Revolution.

_____ 11. The discovery of gold in California was the beginning of the event known as the Gold Rush.

_____ 12. Colonists grew tobacco in Jamestown.

_____ 13. Sacagawea was a Native American woman on the Lewis and Clark Expedition.

_____ 14. Freedom of the press is the most important right granted to citizens by the United States Constitution.

_____ 15. British soldiers in the American Revolution deserved the nickname "Redcoats."

The First Amendment

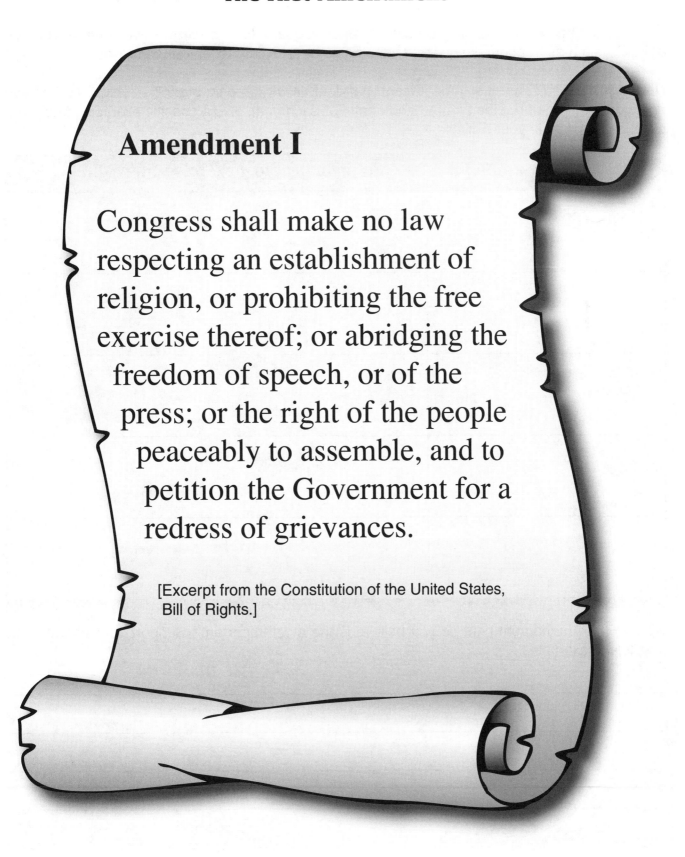

Amendment I

Congress shall make no law respecting an establishment of religion, or prohibiting the free exercise thereof; or abridging the freedom of speech, or of the press; or the right of the people peaceably to assemble, and to petition the Government for a redress of grievances.

[Excerpt from the Constitution of the United States, Bill of Rights.]

Name: _____ Date: _____

Exercising My First Amendment Freedoms

Amendment I of the United States Constitution guarantees its citizens five personal liberties or rights, such as freedom of speech. These rights have an impact on our daily lives.

Directions: Read "The First Amendment" handout. In the graphic organizer below, list the five rights guaranteed under the First Amendment. For each right, give a specific example of how you exercise this right in your daily life.

First Amendment Right	In my daily life, I exercise this right . . .

Which First Amendment right do you believe is the most important? Support your answer with details and examples.

_____

_____

_____

_____

Name: _____ Date: _____

William Clark's Journal Entry

Incomplete sentences and misspellings are common mistakes in the journal entries of William Clark. In 1805, Meriwether Lewis sent a portion of Clark's private journal back to Thomas Jefferson from Fort Mandan. In his April 7th letter to President Jefferson, Meriwether Lewis stated, "Capt. Clark does not wish this journal exposed in its present state, but has no objection, that one or more copies of it be made by some confidential person under your direction, correcting its grammatical errors."

Directions: Access the journals of the Lewis and Clark Expedition at the URL below. Follow the steps to locate William Clark's journal entry for April 1, 1805. Rewrite Clark's first journal entry for that day using correct grammar, sentence structure, and spelling.

Step 1: Go online to the URL: <**http://lewisandclarkjournals.unl.edu/**>.
Step 2: Click on **Read the Journals** link.
Step 3: Under **1805** click on the **April** link.

April 1, 1805

_____

_____

_____

_____

_____

_____

_____

_____

_____

_____

_____

_____

_____

Pioneers on the Western Trails

Randolph Marcy was a career soldier in the United States Army, a Western explorer, and an expedition leader. He used his experiences to write his book, *The Prairie Traveler: A Handbook for Overland Expeditions with Maps, Illustrations, and Itineraries of the Principal Routes between the Mississippi and the Pacific*. Published in 1859, his book became a vital handbook for pioneers navigating the western trails.

A suitable dress for prairie traveling is of great import to health and comfort. Cotton or linen fabrics do not sufficiently protect the body against the direct rays of the sun at midday, nor against rains or sudden changes of temperature. Wool, being a non-conductor, is the best material for this mode of locomotion, and should always be adopted for the plains. The coat should be short and stout, the shirt of red or blue flannel, such as can be found in almost all the shops on the frontier: this, in warm weather, answers for an outside garment. The pants should be of thick and soft woolen material, and it is well to have them re-enforced on the inside, where they come in contact with the saddle, with soft buckskin, which makes them more durable and comfortable.

Woolen socks and stout boots, coming up well at the knees, and made large, so as to admit the pants, will be found the best for horsemen, and they guard against rattlesnake bites.

In traveling through deep snow during very cold weather in winter, moccasins are preferable to boots or shoes, as being more pliable, and allowing a freer circulation of the blood. In crossing the Rocky Mountains in the winter, the weather being intensely cold, I wore two pairs of woolen socks, and a square piece of thick blanket sufficient to cover the feet and ankles, over which were drawn a pair of thick buckskin moccasins, and the whole enveloped in a pair of buffalo-skin boots with the hair inside, made open in the front and tied with buckskin strings. At the same time I wore a pair of elkskin pants, which most effectually prevented the air from penetrating to the skin, and made an excellent defense against brush and thorns.

My men, who were dressed in the regulation clothing, wore out their pants and shoes before we reached the summit of the mountains, and many of them had their feet badly frozen in consequence. They mended their shoes with pieces of leather cut from the saddle-skirts as long as they lasted, and, when this material was gone, they covered the entire shoe with green beeve or mule hide, drawn together and sewed upon the top, with the hair inside, which protected the upper as well as the sole leather. The sewing was done with an awl and buckskin strings. These simple expedients contributed greatly to the comfort of the party; and, indeed, I am by no means sure that they did not, in our straitened condition, without the transportation necessary for carrying disabled men, save the lives of some of them. Without the awl and buckskins we should have been unable to have repaired the shoes. They should never be forgotten in making up the outfit for a prairie expedition.

Pioneers on the Western Trails (cont.)

We also experienced great inconvenience and pain by the reflection of the sun's rays from the snow upon our eyes, and some of the party became nearly snow-blind. Green or blue glasses, inclosed in a wire net-work, are an effectual protection to the eyes; but, in the absence of these, the skin around the eyes and upon the nose should be blackened with wet powder or charcoal, which will afford great relief.

In the summer season shoes are much better for footmen than boots, as they are lighter, and do not cramp the ankles; the soles should be broad, so as to allow a square, firm tread, without distorting or pinching the feet.

The following list of articles is deemed a sufficient outfit for one man upon a three months' expedition, viz.:

- 2 blue or red flannel overshirts, open in front, with buttons.
- 2 woolen undershirts.
- 2 pairs thick cotton drawers.
- 4 pairs woolen socks.
- 2 pairs cotton socks.
- 4 colored silk handkerchiefs.
- 2 pairs stout shoes, for footmen.
- 1 pair boots, for horsemen.
- 1 pair shoes, for horsemen.
- 3 towels.
- 1 gutta percha poncho.
- 1 broad-brimmed hat of soft felt.
- 1 comb and brush.
- 2 tooth-brushes.
- 1 pound Castile soap.
- 3 pounds bar soap for washing clothes.
- 1 belt-knife and small whetstone.
- Stout linen thread, large needles, a bit of beeswax, a few buttons, paper of pins, and a thimble, all contained in a small buckskin or stout cloth bag.

The foregoing articles, with the coat and overcoat, complete the wardrobe.

[Excerpt from *Prairie Traveler: A Hand-Book for Overland Expeditions, . . .* by Randolph B. Marcy, 1859. Capitalization, punctuation, and spelling are as found in the original document.]

Name: _____ Date: _____

Clothing for Prairie Travelers

Directions: Read the "Pioneers on the Western Trails" handout and answer the following questions. Support your answers with textual evidence.

1. Why was it important to wear "suitable dress" when traveling across the prairie?

    _____

    _____

    _____

2. Why would a wool coat be a better choice for a prairie traveler than a coat made of cotton fabric?

    _____

    _____

    _____

3. How did the footwear needed for "traveling through deep snow" differ from the recommended summer footwear?

    _____

    _____

4. Why were buckskins and an awl necessary items for the prairie traveler?

    _____

    _____

5. Marcy told about the necessary clothing items needed for an overland expedition. He also included a list of supplies needed for "one man upon a three months' expedition." Which clothing item told about in the excerpt was not listed?

    _____

    _____

Extended Learning Activity

To access an online copy of Randolph Marcy's book, go online to the following URL: <**http://www.kancoll.org/books/marcy/**>.

The Emancipation Proclamation [Transcript]

By the President of the United States of America:

A Proclamation.

Whereas, on the twenty-second day of September, in the year of our Lord one thousand eight hundred and sixty-two, a proclamation was issued by the President of the United States, containing, among other things, the following, to wit:

"That on the first day of January, in the year of our Lord one thousand eight hundred and sixty-three, all persons held as slaves within any State or designated part of a State, the people whereof shall then be in rebellion against the United States, shall be then, thenceforward, and forever free; and the Executive Government of the United States, including the military and naval authority thereof, will recognize and maintain the freedom of such persons, and will do no act or acts to repress such persons, or any of them, in any efforts they may make for their actual freedom.

"That the Executive will, on the first day of January aforesaid, by proclamation, designate the States and parts of States, if any, in which the people thereof, respectively, shall then be in rebellion against the United States; and the fact that any State, or the people thereof, shall on that day be, in good faith, represented in the Congress of the United States by members chosen thereto at elections wherein a majority of the qualified voters of such State shall have participated, shall, in the absence of strong countervailing testimony, be deemed conclusive evidence that such State, and the people thereof, are not then in rebellion against the United States."

Now, therefore I, Abraham Lincoln, President of the United States, by virtue of the power in me vested as Commander-in-Chief, of the Army and Navy of the United States in time of actual armed rebellion against the authority and government of the United States, and as a fit and necessary war measure for suppressing said rebellion, do, on this first day of January, in the year of our Lord one thousand eight hundred and sixty-three, and in accordance with my purpose so to do publicly proclaimed for the full period of one hundred days, from the day first above mentioned, order and designate as the States and parts of States wherein the people thereof respectively, are this day in rebellion against the United States, the following, to wit:

Arkansas, Texas, Louisiana, (except the Parishes of St. Bernard, Plaquemines, Jefferson, St. John, St. Charles, St. James Ascension, Assumption, Terrebonne, Lafourche, St. Mary, St. Martin, and Orleans, including the City of New Orleans) Mississippi, Alabama, Florida, Georgia, South Carolina, North Carolina, and Virginia, (except the forty-eight counties designated as West Virginia, and also the counties of Berkley, Accomac, Northampton, Elizabeth City, York, Princess Ann, and Norfolk, including the cities of Norfolk and Portsmouth[)], and which excepted parts are, for the present, left precisely as if this proclamation were not issued.

The Emancipation Proclamation (cont.)

And by virtue of the power, and for the purpose aforesaid, I do order and declare that all persons held as slaves within said designated States, and parts of States, are, and henceforward shall be free; and that the Executive government of the United States, including the military and naval authorities thereof, will recognize and maintain the freedom of said persons.

And I hereby enjoin upon the people so declared to be free to abstain from all violence, unless in necessary self-defence; and I recommend to them that, in all cases when allowed, they labor faithfully for reasonable wages.

And I further declare and make known, that such persons of suitable condition, will be received into the armed service of the United States to garrison forts, positions, stations, and other places, and to man vessels of all sorts in said service.

And upon this act, sincerely believed to be an act of justice, warranted by the Constitution, upon military necessity, I invoke the considerate judgment of mankind, and the gracious favor of Almighty God.

In witness whereof, I have hereunto set my hand and caused the seal of the United States to be affixed.

Done at the city of Washington, this first day of January, in the year of our Lord one thousand eight hundred and sixty three, and of the Independence of the United States of America the eighty-seventh.

{seal}

Abraham Lincoln

By the President:

William H. Seward
Secretary of State.

[Capitalization, punctuation, and spelling are as found in the original document. The original document does show quotation marks before each line of the first and second paragraph. These marks have been left off this transcript to aid readability.]

Name: _____ Date: _____

The President Makes a Proclamation

Directions: Read "The Emancipation Proclamation" handout and answer the following questions. Cite textual evidence to support your answers.

1. Who issued the proclamation?

    _____

    _____

    _____

2. What was the purpose of the proclamation?

    _____

    _____

    _____

    _____

    _____

    _____

3. According to the proclamation, what actions were to be required of the military and naval authority?

    _____

    _____

    _____

    _____

    _____

Name: _____ Date: _____

The President Makes a Proclamation (cont.)

4. What two reasons did Abraham Lincoln state as his authority for issuing the proclamation?

_____

_____

_____

_____

5. What two actions did Lincoln encourage the freed slaves to take?

_____

_____

_____

6. Were freed slaves allowed to join the military? _____

_____

_____

7. What justification did Lincoln give for believing the proclamation "to be an act of justice"?

_____

_____

_____

Extended Learning Activity

Conduct research about the reaction of blacks living in Union states and those living in the rebellious states upon hearing about the Emancipation Proclamation.

Lincoln's Letter to Mrs. Bixby

The original letter that Abraham Lincoln wrote to Mrs. Bixby no longer exists. However, a copy was printed in a Boston newspaper a few days after being delivered to Mrs. Bixby. There is controversy concerning whether Abraham Lincoln or one of his aides wrote the letter.

Executive Mansion,
Washington , November 21, 1864

To Mrs. Bixby, Boston, Mass.

Dear Madam,

I have been shown in the files of the War Department a statement of the Adjutant General of Massachusetts that you are the mother of five sons who have died gloriously on the field of battle. I feel how weak and fruitless must be any word of mine which should attempt to beguile you from the grief of a loss so overwhelming. But I cannot refrain from tendering you the consolation that may be found in the thanks of the republic they died to save. I pray that our Heavenly Father may assuage the anguish of your bereavement, and leave you only the cherished memory of the loved and lost, and the solemn pride that must be yours to have laid so costly a sacrifice upon the altar of freedom.

Yours, very sincerely and respectfully,

A. Lincoln

Name: _____   Date: _____

A Letter of Consolation

Directions: Read the "Lincoln's Letter to Mrs. Bixby" handout and answer the following questions. Support your answers with textual evidence.

1. Where and when was the letter written? _____

_____

_____

2. Where did Mrs. Bixby live? _____

_____

3. How many sons of Mrs. Bixby died in the war? _____

_____

_____

4. Which war was taking place when Lincoln wrote his letter to Mrs. Bixby? _____

_____

_____

5. What was Lincoln's purpose for writing the letter? _____

_____

_____

_____

6. How did Lincoln describe the words he used to console Mrs. Bixby? _____

_____

_____

7. Which two things did Lincoln hope would lessen Mrs. Bixby's bereavement over the loss of her sons?

_____

_____

_____

_____

America the Beautiful

O beautiful for spacious skies,
For amber waves of grain,
For purple mountain majesties
Above the fruited plain!
America! America! God shed His grace on thee,
And crown thy good with brotherhood
From sea to shining sea!

O beautiful for pilgrim feet,
Whose stern, impassion'd stress
A thoroughfare for freedom beat
Across the wilderness!
America! America! God mend thine ev'ry flaw,
Confirm thy soul in self-control,
Thy liberty in law!

O beautiful for heroes proved in liberating strife,
Who more than self their country loved,
And mercy more than life!
America! America! May God thy gold refine
Till all success be nobleness,
And ev'ry gain divine!

O Beautiful for patriot dream
That sees beyond the years
Thine alabaster cities gleam,
Undimmed by human tears!
America! America! God shed His grace on thee,
And crown thy good with brotherhood
From sea to shining sea!

Katherine Lee Bates

Name: _____ Date: _____

Word Meaning

Directions: Read the "America the Beautiful" handout. Use a print or online dictionary to find the meaning of each word as it is used in the poem.

Word	Meaning
1. amber	
2. fruited	
3. thoroughfare	
4. confirm	
5. alabaster	

Extended Learning Activity

Almost every line of the poem suggests a mental picture. Create a multimedia presentation illustrating the visual imagery of the poem.

Name: _____ Date: _____

Interpreting a Poem

First published as a poem, the words to "America the Beautiful" were later set to music. This song is sometimes referred to as the national hymn of the United States.

Directions: Read the "America the Beautiful" handout. Answer the questions. Cite textual evidence to support your answers.

1. What was the author's purpose for writing the poem?

   _____

   _____

   _____

2. What is the tone of the poem?

   _____

   _____

   _____

3. What is the theme of the first stanza of the poem?

   _____

   _____

   _____

4. A hymn is a religious song of praise or joy. Cite evidence from the poem that supports the idea that "America the Beautiful" can be considered a hymn.

   _____

   _____

   _____

   _____

Child Labor in a Textile Mill, 1909

Library of Congress <http://www.loc.gov/pictures/item/ncl2004001430/PP/>

Name: _____   Date: _____

Analyzing a Photograph

Directions: Study the photograph on the "Child Labor in a Textile Mill, 1909" handout. Use your observations to answer the following questions.

1. Describe the appearance of the boy in the photograph, including approximate age, clothing, and facial expressions.

   _____

   _____

   _____

   _____

   _____

2. What job does the boy appear to be doing in the photograph?

   _____

   _____

   _____

3. Based on your observations, what does the photograph tell you about this time period?

   _____

   _____

   _____

   _____

Extended Learning Activity

To access the National Child Labor Committee Collection of photographs at the Library of Congress go online to the following URL: **<http://www.loc.gov/pictures/collection/nclc/>**.

Woodrow Wilson's Press Statement [Transcript]

In 1917, the United States War Department formed the National Army to fight in World War I. The Army was made up of the Regular Army, the National Guard, and draftees. President Woodrow Wilson released the following press statement to the soldiers in the National Army who were leaving for France.

To the Soldiers of the National Army:

You are undertaking a great duty. The heart of the whole country is with you. Everything that you do will be watched with the deepest interest and with the deepest solicitude not only by those who are near and dear to you, but by the whole nation besides. For this great war draws us all closer together, makes us all comrades and brothers, as all true Americans felt themselves to be when we first made good our national independence. The eyes of all the world will be upon you, because you are in some special sense the soldiers of freedom. Let it be your pride, therefore, to show all men everywhere not only what good soldiers you are, keeping yourselves fit and straight in everything and pure and clean through and through. Let us set for ourselves a standard so high that it will be a glory to live up to it and then let us live up to it and add a new laurel to the crown of America. My affectionate confidence goes with you in every battle and every test. God keep and guide you!

WOODROW WILSON

7 August, 1917

The White House

Washington

Name: _____ Date: _____

To the Soldiers of the National Army

Directions: Read the "Woodrow Wilson's Press Statement" handout. Answer the following questions. Cite textual evidence to support your answers.

1. Who was the intended audience?

   _____

   _____

   _____

2. What was President Wilson's purpose for issuing the statement?

   _____

   _____

   _____

   _____

   _____

3. For what purpose were the "soldiers of freedom" encouraged to be "good soldiers"?

   _____

   _____

   _____

   _____

   _____

4. How did President Wilson compare "this great war" to the Revolutionary War?

   _____

   _____

   _____

   _____

World War I

The following is the text-only portion from a World War I poster. The poster can be viewed in its entirety at the URL: <**http://hdl.loc.gov/pictures/resources/cph.3g09934**>.

Shoot Ships to Germany and
help AMERICA WIN—Schwab

At this Shipyard are being built ships to carry to
our men "Over There"—Food, Clothing, and the
Munitions of War.

Without these ships our men will not have an equal
chance to fight.

The building of ships is more than
a construction job—it is our chance to win the war.

He who gives to his work the best that is in him does
his bit as truly as the man who fights.

Delays mean danger.
    Are you doing your bit?

Are you giving the best that is in you to help your
son, brother, or pal who is "OVER THERE"?

Name: _____ Date: _____

Help America Win!

On April 6, 1917, America officially announced that it was declaring war against Germany. This news inspired George M. Cohan to write the song "Over There." It became one of the most famous songs of World War I.

Directions: Read the "World War I" handout. Answer the following questions. Cite textual evidence to support your answers.

1. Who was the intended audience?

   _____

   _____

   _____

2. What was the message?

   _____

   _____

   _____

3. What was the purpose of the poster?

   _____

   _____

   _____

4. How might the poster have influenced the people who read it?

   _____

   _____

   _____

The Birth of Freedom

Directions: Read Documents A and B. Answer the questions that follow. Cite textual evidence to support your answers.

Document A: The Declaration of Independence [Transcript]

In CONGRESS. July 4, 1776.

The unanimous Declaration of the thirteen united States of America.

Introduction

When in the Course of human events, it becomes necessary for one people to dissolve the political bands which have connected them with another, and to assume, among the Powers of the earth, the separate and equal station to which the Laws of Nature and of Nature's God entitle them, a decent respect to the opinions of mankind requires that they should declare the causes which impel them to the separation.

Rights

We hold these truths to be self-evident, that all men are created equal, that they are endowed by their Creator with certain unalienable Rights, that among these are Life, Liberty, and the pursuit of Happiness. That to secure these rights, Governments are instituted among Men, deriving their just Powers from the consent of the governed. That, whenever any form of Government becomes destructive of these ends, it is the Right of the People to alter or to abolish it, and to institute new Government, laying its foundation on such Principles, and organizing its Powers in such form, as to them shall seem most likely to effect their Safety and Happiness. Prudence, indeed, will dictate that Governments long established should not be changed for light and transient causes; and, accordingly, all experience hath shewn, that mankind are more disposed to suffer, while evils are sufferable, than to right themselves by abolishing the forms to which they are accustomed. But, when a long train of abuses and usurpations, pursuing invariably the same Object, evinces a design to reduce them under absolute Despotism, it is their right, it is their duty, to throw off such Government, and to provide new Guards for their future security. Such has been the patient sufferance of these Colonies; and such is now the necessity which constrains them to alter their former Systems of Government. The history of the present King of Great Britain is a history of repeated injuries and usurpations, all having in direct object the establishment of an absolute Tyranny over these States. To prove this, let Facts be submitted to a candid world.

Grievances

He has refused his Assent to Laws, the most wholesome and necessary for the public good.

He has forbidden his Governors to pass Laws of immediate and pressing importance, unless suspended in their operation till his Assent should be obtained; and when so suspended, he has utterly neglected to attend to them.

He has refused to pass other Laws for the accommodation of large districts of People, unless those People would relinquish the right of Representation in the Legislature; a right inestimable to them and formidable to tyrants only.

Document A: The Declaration of Independence [Transcript] (cont.)

Grievances (continued)

He has called together legislative bodies at places unusual, uncomfortable, and distant from the depository of their Public Records, for the sole Purpose of fatiguing them into compliance with his measures.

He has dissolved Representative Houses repeatedly, for opposing with manly firmness his invasions on the rights of the People.

He has refused for a long time, after such dissolutions, to cause others to be elected; whereby the Legislative Powers, incapable of Annihilation, have returned to the People at large for their exercise; the State remaining in the mean time exposed to all the dangers of invasion from without, and convulsions within.

He has endeavoured to prevent the Population of these States; for that purpose obstructing the Laws for Naturalization of Foreigners; refusing to pass others to encourage their migrations hither, and raising the conditions of new Appropriations of Lands.

He has obstructed the Administration of Justice, by refusing his Assent to Laws for establishing Judiciary powers.

He has made Judges dependent on his Will alone, for the tenure of their offices, and the amount and payment of their salaries.

He has erected a multitude of New Offices, and sent hither swarms of Officers to harrass our people, and eat out their substance.

He has kept among us, in times of Peace, Standing Armies without the Consent of our legislatures.

He has affected to render the Military independent of and superior to the Civil Power.

He has combined with others to subject us to a jurisdiction foreign to our constitution, and unacknowledged by our laws; giving his Assent to their Acts of pretended Legislation:

For Quartering large bodies of armed troops among us:

For protecting them, by a mock Trial, from Punishment for any Murders which they should commit on the Inhabitants of these States:

For cutting off our Trade with all parts of the world:

For imposing Taxes on us without our Consent:

For depriving us, in many cases, of the benefits of Trial by Jury:

For transporting us beyond Seas to be tried for pretended offences:

For abolishing the free System of English Laws in a neighbouring province, establishing therein an Arbitrary government, and enlarging its Boundaries, so as to render it at once an example and fit instrument for introducing the same absolute rule into these Colonies:

For taking away our Charters, abolishing our most valuable Laws, and altering fundamentally the Forms of our Governments:

For suspending our own Legislatures, and declaring themselves invested with Power to legislate for us in all cases whatsoever.

He has abdicated Government here, by declaring us out of his protection and waging War against us.

He has plundered our seas, ravaged our Coasts, burnt our towns, and destroyed the Lives of our People.

Document A: The Declaration of Independence [Transcript]

Grievances (continued)

He is at this time transporting large Armies of foreign Mercenaries to compleat the works of death, desolation and tyranny, already begun with circumstances of Cruelty and perfidy scarcely paralleled in the most barbarous ages, and totally unworthy the Head of a civilized nation.

He has constrained our fellow Citizens taken Captive on the high Seas to bear Arms against their Country, to become the executioners of their friends and Brethren, or to fall themselves by their Hands.

He has excited domestic insurrections amongst us, and has endeavoured to bring on the inhabitants of our frontiers, the merciless Indian Savages, whose known rule of warfare, is an undistinguished destruction of all ages, sexes and conditions.

In every stage of these Oppressions, We have Petitioned for Redress in the most humble terms: Our repeated Petitions have been answered only by repeated injury. A Prince whose character is thus marked by every act which may define a Tyrant, is unfit to be the ruler of a free people.

Nor have We been wanting in attentions to our Brittish brethren. We have warned them from time to time of attempts by their legislature to extend an unwarrantable jurisdiction over us. We have reminded them of the circumstances of our emigration and settlement here. We have appealed to their native justice and magnanimity, and we have conjured them by the ties of our common kindred, to disavow these usurpations, which, would inevitably interrupt our connexions and correspondence. They too have been deaf to the voice of justice and of consanguinity. We must, therefore, acquiesce in the necessity, which denounces our Separation, and hold them, as we hold the rest of mankind, Enemies in War, in Peace Friends.

Conclusion

We, therefore, the REPRESENTATIVES of the united States of America, in GENERAL CONGRESS Assembled, appealing to the Supreme Judge of the World for the rectitude of our intentions, DO, in the Name, and by Authority of the good People of these Colonies, solemnly PUBLISH and DECLARE, That these United Colonies are, and of Right ought to be Free and Independent States; that they are Absolved from all Allegiance to the British Crown, and that all political connexion between them and the State of Great Britain, is and ought to be totally dissolved; and, that as FREE and INDEPENDENT STATES, they have full Power to levy War, conclude Peace, contract Alliances, establish Commerce, and to do all other Acts and Things which INDEPENDENT STATES may of right do. AND for the support of this Declaration, with a firm reliance on the protection of divine Providence, we mutually pledge to each other our Lives, our Fortunes, and our sacred Honour.

Signers

The foregoing declaration was, by order of Congress, engrossed, and signed by the following members:

[The names of the signers to the Declaration are listed on the original document, but they are not included in this transcription.]

[Excerpt from the *Journals of the Continental Congress 1774–1789*. Volume V. 1776. pages 509–515, located at the Library of Congress website.]

The Birth of Freedom (cont.)

Document B: Letter. John Adams' Letter to Abigail Adams, July 3, 1776

The excerpt below was taken from a letter written by John Adams to his wife, Abigail. In the letter, Adams discusses the resolution to write the document now known as the Declaration of Independence.

> Yesterday, the greatest question was decided, which ever was debated in America, and a greater, perhaps, never was nor will be decided among men. A resolution was passed without one dissenting colony, "that these United Colonies are, and of right ought to be, free and independent States, and as such they have, and of right ought to have, full power to make war, conclude peace, establish commerce, and to do all other acts and things which other States may rightfully do." You will see in a few days a Declaration setting forth the causes which have impelled us to this mighty revolution, and the reasons which will justify it in the sight of God and man. A plan of confederation will be taken up in a few days.
>
> You will think me transported with enthusiasm, but I am not. I am well aware of the toil, and blood, and treasure, that it will cost us to maintain this declaration, and support and defend these States. Yet, through all the gloom, I can see the rays of ravishing light and glory. I can see that the end is more than worth all the means, and that posterity will triumph in that day's transaction, even although we should rue it, which I trust in God we shall not.

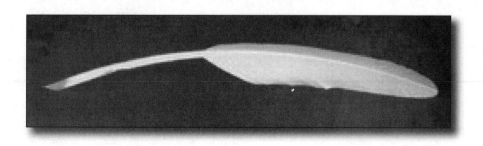

Name: _____   Date: _____

Learning Activity: The Birth of Freedom

Use Document A to answer question 1.

1. Summarize in your own words the following sections of the Declaration of Independence.

Section	Summary
Introduction	
Rights	
Grievances	
Conclusion	

Name: _____ Date: _____

Learning Activity: The Birth of Freedom (cont.)

Use Document B to answer questions 2–4.

2. What importance did John Adams place on the passing of the resolution?

Abigail and John Adams

_____

_____

_____

_____

_____

_____

_____

3. What two pieces of information did Adams say the Declaration would include?

_____

_____

_____

_____

_____

_____

4. How did John Adams feel about independence being declared?

_____

_____

_____

_____

_____

Name: _____   Date: _____

Learning Activity: The Birth of Freedom (cont.)

> **Use Documents A and B to answer questions 5–7.**

5. Adams stated that the Declaration of Independence would present reasons which "justify it in the sight of God and man." List the two reasons stated in the Declaration of Independence that the writer felt justified the revolution.

_____

_____

_____

6. Adams stated "you will see in a few days a Declaration setting forth the causes which have impelled us to this mighty revolution." Examine the Declaration of Independence and list four of the causes to which Adams was referring.

_____

_____

_____

_____

7. In his letter, Adams stated, "I am well aware of the toil, and blood, and treasure, that it will cost us to maintain this declaration, and support and defend these States." What textual evidence from the conclusion of the Declaration of Independence supports this statement?

_____

_____

_____

Extended Learning Activity

Go online to the URL: <http://www.archives.gov/exhibits/charters/ declaration_sign. html>. Click on the **Join the Signers of the Declaration** link and add your signature to a copy of this historical document.

Name: _____   Date: _____

Learning Activity: Dear Mrs. Roosevelt

During the years of the Great Depression, First Lady Eleanor Roosevelt received many letters from children and youth. The letters requested help with money, clothes, and luxuries.

Directions: Access the "Dear Mrs. Roosevelt" Website at the URL below. Follow the steps to locate transcripts of some of the letters written to Mrs. Roosevelt. There are four categories of letters. Select two letters. Each letter must be from a different category.

Step 1: Go online to the URL: <**http://newdeal.feri.org/eleanor/**>.
Step 2: Click on **The Letters** link.
Step 3: Click on the **Requests for . . .** links to access the letters under the four categories.

Letter One
1. Who wrote the letter and where did they live?
2. When was the letter written?
3. In your own words, summarize the letter.

Letter Two
1. Who wrote the letter and where did they live?
2. When was the letter written?
3. In your own words, summarize the letter.

Based on Letters One and Two, what can you infer about the life of children and youth during the Great Depression? Cite textual evidence to support your answer.

_____

_____

_____

_____

World War II

Directions: Read Documents A and B. Answer the questions that follow. Cite textual evidence to support your answers.

Document A: Executive Order No. 9066 [Transcript]

EXECUTIVE ORDER

AUTHORIZING THE SECRETARY OF WAR TO PRESCRIBE MILITARY AREAS

WHEREAS the successful prosecution of the war requires every possible protection against espionage and against sabotage to national-defense material, national-defense premises, and national-defense utilities as defined in Section 4, Act of April 20, 1918, 40 Stat. 533, as amended by the Act of November 30, 1940, 54 Stat. 1220, and the Act of August 21, 1941, 55 Stat. 655 (U.S.C., Title 50, Sec. 104);

NOW, THEREFORE, by virtue of the authority vested in me as President of the United States, and Commander in Chief of the Army and Navy, I hereby authorize and direct the Secretary of War, and the Military Commanders whom he may from time to time designate, whenever he or any designated Commander deems such action necessary or desirable, to prescribe military areas in such places and of such extent as he or the appropriate Military Commander may determine, from which any or all persons may be excluded, and with respect to which, the right of any person to enter, remain in, or leave shall be subject to whatever restrictions the Secretary of War or the appropriate Military Commander may impose in his discretion. The Secretary of War is hereby authorized to provide for residents of any such area who are excluded therefrom, such transportation, food, shelter, and other accommodations as may be necessary, in the judgment of the Secretary of War or the said Military Commander, and until other arrangements are made, to accomplish the purpose of this order. The designation of military areas in any region or locality shall supersede designations of prohibited and restricted areas by the Attorney General under the Proclamations of December 7 and 8, 1941, and shall supersede the responsibility and authority of the Attorney General under the said Proclamations in respect of such prohibited and restricted areas.

I hereby further authorize and direct the Secretary of War and the said Military Commanders to take such other steps as he or the appropriate Military Commander may deem advisable to enforce compliance with the restrictions applicable to each Military area herein above authorized to be designated, including the use of Federal troops and other Federal Agencies, with authority to accept assistance of state and local agencies.

I hereby further authorize and direct all Executive Departments, independent establishments and other Federal Agencies, to assist the Secretary of War or the said Military Commanders in carrying out this Executive Order, including the furnishing of medical aid, hospitalization, food, clothing, transportation, use of land, shelter, and other supplies, equipment, utilities, facilities, and services.

This order shall not be construed as modifying or limiting in any way the authority heretofore granted under Executive Order No. 8972, dated December 12, 1941, nor shall it be construed as limiting or modifying the duty and responsibility of the Federal Bureau of Investigation, with respect to the investigation of alleged acts of sabotage or the duty and responsibility of the Attorney General and the Department of Justice under the Proclamations of December 7 and 8, 1941, prescribing regulations for the conduct and control of alien enemies, except as such duty and responsibility is superseded by the designation of military areas hereunder.

Franklin D. Roosevelt
February 19, 1942

World War II (cont.)

Document B: Public Law 100-383 [Excerpt]

One hundredth Congress of the United States of America
AT THE SECOND SESSION

Begun and held at the City of Washington on Monday, the twenty-fifth day of January, one thousand nine hundred and eighty-eight

An Act

To implement recommendations of the Commission on Wartime Relocation and Internment of Civilians.

Be it enacted by the Senate and House of Representatives of the United States of America in Congress assembled,

SECTION 1. PURPOSES.

The purpose of this Act are to—

(1) acknowledge the fundamental injustice of the evacuation, relocation, and internment of United Sates citizens and permanent resident aliens of Japanese ancestry during World War II;

(2) apologize on behalf of the people of the United States for the evacuation, relocation, and internment of such citizens and permanent resident aliens;

(3) provide for public education fund to finance efforts to inform the public about the internment of such individuals so as to prevent the recurrence of any similar event;

(4) make restitution to those individuals of Japanese ancestry who were interned . . .

(5) discourage the occurrence of similar injustices and violations of civil liberties in the future; and

(6) make more credible and sincere any declaration of concern by the United States over violations of human rights committed by other nations.

SECT. 2. STATEMENT OF THE CONGRESS.

(a) WITH REGARD TO INDIVIDUALS OF JAPANESE ANCESTRY.—The Congress recognizes that, as described by the Commission on Wartime Relocation and Internment of Civilians, a grave injustice was done to both citizens and permanent resident aliens of Japanese ancestry by the evacuation, relocation, and internment of civilians during World War II. As the Commission documents, these actions were carried out without adequate security reasons and without any acts of espionage or sabotage documented by the Commission, and were motivated largely by racial prejudice, wartime hysteria, and a failure of political leadership. The excluded individuals of Japanese ancestry suffered enormous damages, both material and intangible, and there were incalculable losses in education and job training, all of which resulted in significant human suffering for which appropriate compensation has not been made. For these fundamental violations of the basic civil liberties and constitutional rights of these individuals of Japanese ancestry, the Congress apologizes on behalf of the nation.

Name: _____ Date: _____

Learning Activity: Japanese-American Relocation and Internment

Use Document A to answer questions 1–4.

Gila River Relocation Center, Rivers, Arizona

1. According to paragraph one, what did "the successful prosecution of the war" require?

   _____

   _____

   _____

   _____

2. According to paragraph two, to whom did the President Roosevelt give authority to set up military areas?

   _____

   _____

   _____

   _____

3. According to paragraph two, what were authorized personnel to determine about people and the military areas?

   _____

   _____

   _____

   _____

4. Why do you think specific ethnic groups were not listed in Executive Order No. 9066?

   _____

   _____

   _____

   _____

Name: _____   Date: _____

Learning Activity: Japanese-American Relocation and Internment (cont.)

Use Document B to answer questions 5–8.

5. Summarize the following purposes of Public Law 100-383.

Purpose	Summary
(1)	
(2)	
(3)	
(4)	
(5)	
(6)	

6. What ethnic group was Congress apologizing to in Section 2(a)?

_____

_____

7. What action was taken against this ethnic group during World War II?

_____

_____

8. What did Congress state as the motivation for the relocation and internment of civilians during World War II?

_____

_____

Name: _____ Date: _____

Learning Activity: Japanese-American Relocation and Internment (cont.)

Use Documents A and B to answer questions 9 and 10.

9. What is the difference between the purposes of Executive Order No. 9066 and Public Law 100-383?

_____

_____

_____

_____

_____

_____

_____

10. How did the perspective for relocation and internment change from 1942 when Executive Order No. 9066 was issued to the issuing of Public Law 100-383 in 1988?

_____

_____

_____

_____

_____

_____

_____

Extended Learning Activity

Go online to the Smithsonian National Museum of American History at the following URL to learn more about the relocation and internment of Japanese-Americans during World War II.

URL: <http://amhistory.si.edu/perfectunion/experience/index.html>

The Dust Bowl

Directions: During the 1930s, the Great Plains region of the United States came to be known as the "Dust Bowl." Examine Document A. Focus on the details of the photograph. Then read Document B. Answer the questions that follow.

Document A: Photograph (Primary Source)

Library of Congress <http://www.loc.gov/pictures/item/2012647036/>

Document B: Living in a Dust Bowl (Secondary Source)

Life had always been difficult for homesteaders on the Great Plains. Farms were small and water scarce with no reservoirs or irrigation systems. Even in good years, many were lucky to break even.

Before farmers moved to the area in the late 1800s, the land was covered with hardy grasses that held the fine-grained soil in place even during times of drought, wind, or torrential rains.

When large numbers of homesteaders settled in the region, they plowed up the grasses and planted crops. The cattle they raised ate whatever grass was left. This exposed the soil to the winds that constantly swept across the flat plains. When a series of droughts hit the area in the early thirties, combined with the farming practices of the past 50 years, there was nothing to hold the soil in place.

A large area in the southern part of the Great Plains region of the United States came to be known as the **Dust Bowl** during the 1930s. Much of this area suffered extensively from soil erosion.

The Depression had already caused the price of wheat and corn to fall to all-time lows. When crops failed, farmers couldn't make mortgage payments on their farms. By 1932, a thousand families a week were losing their farms in Texas, Oklahoma, and Arkansas. Thousands of families migrated west in search of a better life.

In 1935, both the federal and state governments began developing programs to conserve the soil and reclaim the area. This included seeding large areas with grass, crop rotation, contour plowing, terracing, and strip planting. In some areas, "shelter belts" of trees were planted to break the force of the wind.

The problems in the Dust Bowl area increased in 1936 when the winds began blowing almost continuously. People fled to shelter as huge clouds of dust advanced on them. Dust was carried great distances by the wind, in some cases darkening the sky all the way to the Atlantic Ocean.

During the next four years, as much as three to four inches of topsoil blew away, leaving only hard, red clay, which made farming impossible. Sand settled around homes, fences, and barns. People slept with wet cloths over their faces to filter out the dust. They woke to find themselves, their pillows, and blankets caked with dirt. Animals were buried alive or choked to death on the dust.

People died if they remained outside too long during a dust storm. Many also died from what came to be called "dust pneumonia"—severe damage to the lungs caused by breathing dust.

[Adapted from *Industrialization Through the Great Depression* by Cindy Barden and Maria Backus. Used with permission of Mark Twain Media, Inc.]

Name: _____ Date: _____

Learning Activity: Dust Bowl Days

Use Document A, the primary source, to answer question 1.

1. List three details you observed from examining the photograph.

Detail I Observed	This detail makes me wonder about . . .	I think this detail means . . .

Use Document B, the secondary source, to answer question 2.

2. What information did you gain from the secondary source that helped you to better understand the photograph? Cite textual evidence to support your answer.

_____

_____

_____

_____

Extended Learning Activities

Go online to the URL <http://memory.loc.gov/ammem/fsahtml/fahome.html>. Browse the subject index to view photographs showing the results of the devastating dust storms that swept across the Great Plains during the Dust Bowl era.

Go online to the URL <http://www.pbs.org/kenburns/dustbowl/> to explore the Website that accompanies the Ken Burns movie *The Dust Bowl*. Check out the photos, videos, biographies, and the interactive Dust Bowl activities.

Bombing of Pearl Harbor

Directions: Read Document A, the text version of President Franklin Roosevelt's "Day of Infamy" address. Then listen to Document B, the audio version of the speech. Answer the questions that follow. Cite textual evidence to support your answers.

Document A: "Day of Infamy," Address, December 8, 1941 [Transcript]

TO THE CONGRESS OF THE UNITED STATES:

Yesterday, December 7, 1941—a date which will live in infamy—the United States of America was suddenly and deliberately attacked by naval and air forces of the Empire of Japan.

The United States was at peace with that Nation and, at the solicitation of Japan, was still in conversation with its Government and its Emperor looking toward the maintenance of peace in the Pacific. Indeed, one hour after Japanese air squadrons had commenced bombing in Oahu, the Japanese Ambassador to the United States and his colleague delivered to our Secretary of State a formal reply to a recent American message. While this reply stated that it seemed useless to continue the existing diplomatic negotiations, it contained no threat or hint of war or of armed attack.

It will be recorded that the distance of Hawaii from Japan makes it obvious that the attack was deliberately planned many days or even weeks ago. During the intervening time the Japanese Government has deliberately sought to deceive the United States by false statements and expressions of hope for continued peace.

The attack yesterday on the Hawaiian Islands has caused severe damage to American naval and military forces. Very many American lives have been lost. In addition American ships have been reported torpedoed on the high seas between San Francisco and Honolulu.

Yesterday the Japanese Government also launched an attack against Malaya.

Last night Japanese forces attacked Hong Kong.

Last night Japanese forces attacked Guam.

Last night Japanese forces attacked the Philippine Islands.

Last night the Japanese attacked Wake Island. This morning the Japanese attacked Midway Island.

Bombing of Pearl Harbor (cont.)

Document A: "Day of Infamy," Address, December 8, 1941 [Transcript] (continued)

Japan has, therefore, undertaken a surprise offensive extending throughout the Pacific area. The facts of yesterday speak for themselves. The people of the United States have already formed their opinions and well understand the implications to the very life and safety of our nation.

As Commander-in-Chief of the Army and Navy I have directed that all measures be taken for our defense.

Always will be remembered the character of the onslaught against us.

No matter how long it may take us to overcome this premeditated invasion, the American people in their righteous might will win through to absolute victory.

I believe that I interpret the will of the Congress and of the people when I assert that we will not only defend ourselves to the uttermost but will make very certain that this form of treachery shall never endanger us again.

Hostilities exist. There is no blinking at the fact that our people, our territory, and our interests are in grave danger.

With confidence in our armed forces—with the unbounding determination of our people—we will gain the inevitable triumph—so help us God.

I ask that the Congress declare that since the unprovoked and dastardly attack by Japan on Sunday, December seventh, a state of war has existed between the United States and the Japanese Empire.

Franklin D. Roosevelt

THE WHITE HOUSE,

December 8, 1941

Document B: "Day of Infamy" Address, December 8, 1941 [Audio Version]

To access the audio version of President Franklin Roosevelt's "Day of Infamy" address, go online to the National Archives at the following URL:
<**http://research.archives.gov/description/1436350**>.

Name: _____ Date: _____

Learning Activity: War Is Declared!

Use Document A to answer questions 1–7.

1. Type of document (check one):

    ____ newspaper   ____ map

    ____ advertisement   ____ speech/address

    ____ letter   ____ congressional record

    ____ report   ____ newspaper article

    ____ telegram

2. Date of document: _____

3. Who created the document? _____

4. For what audience was the document written? _____

    _____

5. Why was the document written? _____

    _____

6. Is the document a credible source of information? Why or why not? _____

    _____

    _____

    _____

7. What is the central theme of the document? _____

    _____

    _____

    _____

    _____

    _____

Name: _____   Date: _____

Learning Activity: War Is Declared (cont.)

Use Document B to answer question 8.

8. What can you tell about the speaker from his delivery of the speech: voice level, pace, dramatic pause, loaded words, and repetition?

Presentation	Evidence
Voice Level	
Pace	
Dramatic Pause	
Loaded Words	
Repetition	

Use Documents A and B to answer question 9.

9. Did reading the text version of President Roosevelt's speech and then listening to the audio version give you a better understanding of this historical event? Support your answer with details and examples.

_____

_____

_____

_____

Extended Learning Activity

To learn more about the bombing of Pearl Harbor, read one of the following books:
- **Literature:** *Under the Blood Red Sun* by Graham Salisbury
- **Informational Text:** *Pearl Harbor Child: A Child's View of Pearl Harbor from Attack to Peace* by Dorinda Nicholson

Learning Stations Activity: Teacher Page

Title: American Civil War: Characteristics of a Leader

Goal: Students will be able to analyze and interpret primary and secondary sources on the same topic.

Instructions to Teacher

This activity consists of four learning stations. Prior to beginning the station activities, it is important for the teacher to introduce or review with the students the skills of comparing and contrasting, recognizing bias and point of view, identifying word meaning, and making inferences.

Materials List/Setup

Station One: Document A: Autobiographical Sketch of Lincoln (Primary Source)
　　Document B: Biography of Abraham Lincoln (Secondary Source)
　　Activity: Compare and Contrast
Station Two: Document C: Lincoln's Letter to John D. Johnston. November 4, 1851 (Primary Source)
　　Activity: Bias and Point of View
Station Three: Document D: Walt Whitman. Journal Entry, August 12, 1863 (Primary Source)
　　Activity: Word Meaning
Station Four: Document D: Walt Whitman. Journal Entry, August 12, 1863 (Primary Source)
　　Document E: Photograph of Abraham Lincoln (Primary Source)
　　Activity: Making Inferences
Writing Activity
　　Reflection—American Civil War, Characteristics of a Leader
　　Handout: Personality and Character Traits

Activity: one copy per student
Documents: one copy per each student in a group
Handout: one copy per each student in a group

Opening: Discussion Questions (Teacher-Directed)

1. What are primary sources?
2. What are secondary sources?
3. How can primary sources help you to better understand a topic?
4. What are character traits? Personality traits?
5. What do you already know about Abraham Lincoln?
6. What do you know about Lincoln's character or personality?

Student Instructions for Learning Stations

At the learning stations, you will analyze and interpret primary and secondary sources on the topic of Abraham Lincoln. Discuss your answers with other group members after completing each activity.

Closure: Reflection

Students will use the completed learning station activities to help compose the Reflection writing activity.

Document A: Autobiographical Sketch of Lincoln

In his December 20, 1859, letter to J. W. Fell, Abraham Lincoln enclosed a brief autobiographical sketch that Fell had requested. About the sketch, Lincoln wrote in his letter, ". . .There is not much of it, for the reason, I suppose, that there is not much of me—If anything be made out of it, I wish it to be modest, and not to go beyond the material."

I was born Feb. 12, 1809, in Hardin County, Kentucky. My parents were both born in Virginia, of undistinguished families— second families, perhaps I should say— My Mother, who died in my tenth year, was of a family of the name of Hanks, some of whom now reside in Adams, and others in Macon counties, Illinois— My paternal grandfather, Abraham Lincoln, emigrated from Rockingham County, Virginia, to Kentucky about 1781 or 2, when, a year or two later, he was killed by indians, not in battle, but by stealth, when he was laboring to open a farm in the forest— His ancestors, who were quakers, went to Virginia from Berks County, Pennsylvania— An effort to identify them with the New-England family of the same name ended in nothing more definite, than a similarity of Christian names in both families, such as Enoch, Levi, Mordecai, Solomon, Abraham, and the like—

My father, at the death of his father, was but six years of age; and he grew up, litterally without education— He removed from Kentucky to what is now Spencer county, Indiana, in my eighth year— We reached our new home about the time the State came into the Union— It was a wild region, with many bears and other wild animals still in the woods— There I grew up— There were some schools, so called; but no qualification was ever required of a teacher, beyond "readin, writin, and cipherin" to the Rule of Three— If a straggler supposed to understand latin happened to sojourn in the neighborhood, he was looked upon as a wizzard— There was absolutely nothing to excite ambition for education. Of course when I came of age I did not know much— Still somehow, I could read, write, and cipher to the Rule of Three, but that was all— I have not been to school since— The little advance I now have upon this store of education, I have picked up from time to time under the pressure of necessity—

I was raised to farm work, which I continued till I was twenty two— At twenty one I came to Illinois, and passed the first year in Macon County — Then I got to New-Salem (at that time in Sangamon, now in Menard County, where I remained a year as a sort of Clerk in a store— then came the Black-Hawk War; and I was elected a Captain of Volunteers — a success which gave me more pleasure than any I have had since— I went the campaign, was elated, ran for the Legislature the same year (1832) and was beaten — the only time I ever have been beaten by the people— The next, and three succeeding biennial elections, I was elected to the Legislature— I was not a candidate afterwards. During this Legislative period I had studied law, and removed to Springfield to practice it— In 1846 I was once elected to the lower House of Congress— Was not a candidate for re-election— From 1849 to 1854, both inclusive, practiced law more assiduously than ever before— Always a whig in politics, and generally on the whig electoral tickets, making active canvassers— I was losing interest in politics, when the repeal of the Missouri Compromise aroused me again— What I have done since then is pretty well known —

If any personal description of me is thought desirable, it may be said, I am, in height, six feet, four inches, nearly; lean in flesh, weighing, on an average, one hundred and eighty pounds; dark complexion, with coarse black hair, and grey eyes — no other marks or brands recollected—

*Errors in capitalization, punctuation, and spelling are as found in the original document.

Document B: Biography of Abraham Lincoln

Abraham was only nine years old when his mother succumbed to a fatal disease. As she lay on her death-bed she called her son and daughter to her and gave them her last charge. "Be good to one another," she said, "love God and your kin."

The winter which followed was dreary and desolate for the motherless children. A few months later Thomas Lincoln brought to the cabin a second wife who was a mother indeed to the two little ones. She was thrifty and industrious, as well as kind and affectionate, and under her rule the family had more of the comforts of life than it had ever known before. Mrs. Lincoln insisted that ten-year-old Abe must be sent to school and so he trudged every day to the log schoolhouse a mile and a half from home.

He was a diligent student, and he read every book on which he could lay his hands. These books were few in number; the *Bible, Aesop's Fables, Robinson Crusoe, Pilgrim's Progress,* a history of the United States, and Weem's *Life of Washington,* were read and re-read. His bookcase was a crack between the logs of the cabin wall. One night the binding of the *Life of Washington,* was injured by a driving storm; to pay the man from whom it was borrowed for the damage, Abe worked three days in his corn field. At night the boy would lie flat on the floor before the fire and cipher on a plank or a wooden shovel with a piece of charcoal; when the surface was covered with figures, he would erase them and begin anew.

His father considered the hours spent in study as wasted time, and Abe was often called to put his books aside to grub and plow and mow. Such work was little to his taste; he said in later years, "his father taught him to work but never taught him to love work." . . .

In the spring of 1830 when Abe was twenty-one his father moved to Illinois where fertile land was to be had on easy terms. . . . In the new settlement the men set to work to clear away the forest and build cabins. Abe helped to split rails to fence in the little farm. He not only helped at home, but worked for others as occasion demanded. . . .

A little later he made a trip to New Orleans with a boat-load of meat, hogs, and corn. . . . After his return home, he became clerk in a country store. Here by his scrupulous honesty he earned the nickname "Honest Abe." One day he made an overcharge of fourpence and that night he walked several miles to return the money. During his leisure he continued his studies. Books were scarce, and on one occasion he walked six miles to borrow a grammar.

In 1832 Abe Lincoln was elected captain of a company of volunteers who marched with the regular troops against the Indian chief, Black Hawk. Most of the men went home when their term of enlistment expired but Abe Lincoln re-enlisted and served as a private. This was his only experience in actual warfare. When he returned home he presented himself as a candidate for the legislature. His neighbors heartily supported "humble Abraham Lincoln" who was one of them, but he was defeated. He was a clear, straightforward speaker with a pointed, well-told joke for every occasion.

[Excerpt from *Brief Biographies from American History* by Edna Henry Lee Turpin, 1907.]

Document C: Lincoln's Letter to John D. Johnston

November 4, 1851
Shelbyville

Dear Brother, When I came into Charleston day before yesterday, I learned that you are anxious to sell the land where you live and move to Missouri. I have been thinking of this ever since, and cannot but think such a notion is utterly foolish. What can you do in Missouri better than here? Is the land any richer? Can you there, any more than here, raise corn and wheat and oats without work? Will anybody there, any more than here, do your work for you? If you intend to go to work, there is no better place than right where you are; if you do not intend to go to work, you cannot get along anywhere. Squirming and crawling about from place to place can do no good. You have raised no crop this year; and what you really want is to sell the land, get the money, and spend it. Part with the land you have, and, my life upon it, you will never after own a spot big enough to bury you in. Half you will get for the land you will spend in moving to Missouri, and the other half you will eat, drink, and wear out, and no foot of land will be bought. Now, I feel it my duty to have no hand in such a piece of foolery. I feel that it is so even on your own account, and particularly on mother's account. The eastern forty acres I intend to keep for mother while she lives; if you will not cultivate it, it will rent for enough to support her—at least, it will rent for something. Her dower in the other two forties she can let you have, and no thanks to me. Now, do not misunderstand this letter; I do not write it in any unkindness. I write it in order, if possible, to get you to face the truth, which truth is, you are destitute because you have idled away all your time. Your thousand pretences for not getting along better are all nonsense; they deceive nobody but yourself. Go to work is the only cure for your case.

A word to mother. Chapman tells me he wants you to go and live with him. If I were you I would try it awhile. If you get tired of it (as I think you will not), you can return to your own home. Chapman feels very kindly to you, and I have no doubt he will make your situation very pleasant.

[Excerpt from *Speeches & Letters of Abraham Lincoln, 1832-1865*. edited by Merwin Roe. 1912.]

Document D: Walt Whitman. Journal Entry, August 12, 1863

Walt Whitman, a popular American poet, was an admirer of Abraham Lincoln. He lived in Washington, D.C., during the Civil War. Whitman's August 12, 1863, journal entry, published in the book *Specimen Days*, records his sightings of President Lincoln on the streets of Washington D.C.

August 12th.—I see the President almost every day, as I happen to live where he passes to or from his lodgings out of town. He never sleeps at the White House during the hot season, but has **quarters** at a healthy location some three miles north of the city, the Soldiers' home, a United States military establishment. I saw him this morning about 8 1/2 coming in to business, riding on Vermont avenue, near L street. He always has a company of twenty-five or thirty cavalry, with **sabres** drawn and held upright over their shoulders. They say this guard was against his personal wish, but he let his counselors have their way. The party makes no great show in uniform or horses. Mr. Lincoln on the saddle generally rides a good-sized, easy-going gray horse, is dress'd in plain black, somewhat rusty and dusty, wears a black stiff hat, and looks about as ordinary in attire, &c., as the commonest man. A lieutenant, with yellow straps, rides at his left, and following behind, two by two, come the cavalry men, in their yellow-striped jackets. They are generally going at a slow trot, as that is the pace set them by the one they wait upon. The sabres and **accoutrements** clank, and the entirely **unornamental cortège** as it trots towards Lafayette square arouses no sensation, only some curious stranger stops and gazes. I see very plainly ABRAHAM LINCOLN'S dark brown face, with the deep-cut lines, the eyes, always to me with a deep **latent** sadness in the expression. We have got so that we exchange bows, and very cordial ones. Sometimes the President goes and comes in an open **barouche**. The cavalry always accompany him, with drawn sabres. Often I notice as he goes out evenings—and sometimes in the morning, when he returns early—he turns off and halts at the large and handsome residence of the Secretary of War, on K street, and holds conference there. If in his barouche, I can see from my window he does not alight, but sits in his vehicle, and Mr. Stanton comes out to attend him. Sometimes one of his sons, a boy of ten or twelve, accompanies him, riding at his right on a pony. Earlier in the summer I occasionally saw the President and his wife, toward the latter part of the afternoon, out in a barouche, on a pleasure ride through the city. Mrs. Lincoln was dress'd in complete black, with a long **crape** veil. The **equipage** is of the plainest kind, only two horses, and they nothing extra. They pass'd me once very close, and I saw the President in the face fully, as they were moving slowly, and his look, though abstracted, happen'd to be directed steadily in my eye. He bow'd and smiled, but far beneath his smile I noticed well the expression I have alluded to. None of the artists or pictures has caught the deep, though **subtle** and indirect expression of this man's face. There is something else there. One of the great portrait painters of two or three centuries ago is needed.

[Excerpt from *Specimen Days* by Walt Whitman, 1882.]

Document E: Photograph of Abraham Lincoln

This photograph of Abraham Lincoln was taken by Alexander Gardner on November 8, 1863. To view the image online go to the URL: <http://www.loc.gov/pictures/item/96522529/>.

Library of Congress

Name: _____   Date: _____

Learning Station One: Compare and Contrast

Directions: Read Document A, a primary source about Abraham Lincoln, and Document B, a secondary source about Lincoln. Select one of the subtopics listed below. Compare and contrast the information found in the documents about your subtopic.

Subtopics: **Education**   **Military Experience**   **Farm Work**
                 Family   **Political Campaigns**

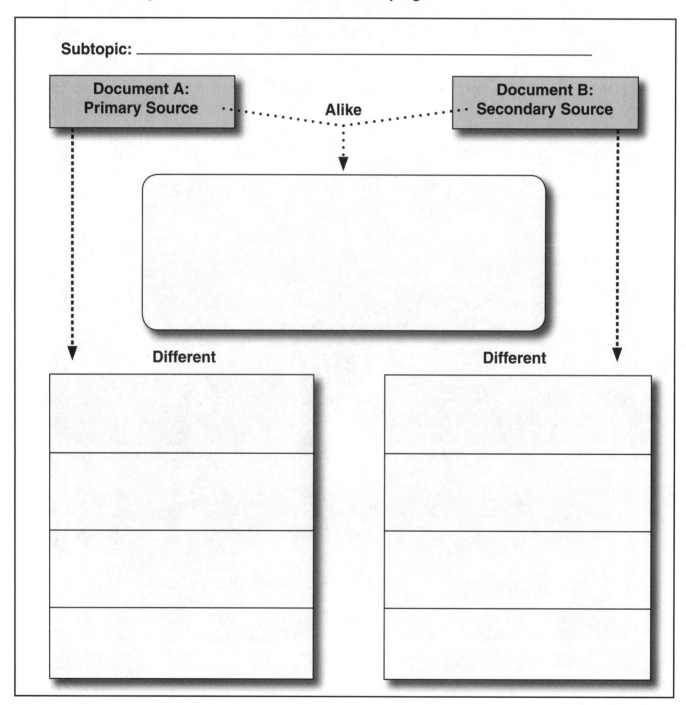

Subtopic: _____

| Document A: Primary Source | Alike | Document B: Secondary Source |

Different   Different

Name: _____ Date: _____

Learning Station Two: Bias and Point of View

Directions: Read Document C, the transcript of a letter Abraham Lincoln sent to his stepbrother, John D. Johnston. Then answer the questions below. Cite textual evidence to support your answer.

1. What was Lincoln's opinion about his brother's decision to sell the land and move to Missouri?

2. What argument did Lincoln make to support his opinion?

3. What emotionally "loaded" words or exaggerations express Lincoln's bias about his brother's decision?

4. What can you infer about Lincoln's opinion of his stepbrother's character?

Name: _____ Date: _____

Learning Station Three: Word Meaning

　　　Primary sources from a historical era may contain unfamiliar or seldom used vocabulary. Not knowing the meaning of words can affect your understanding of a document.

Directions: Read Document D, Walt Whitman's journal entry for August 12, 1863. What do you think each bolded word means? What is the dictionary definition of each bolded word? Record your answers in the graphic organizer.

Word	What You Think the Word Means	Dictionary Definition
1. **quarters**		
2. **sabres**		
3. **accoutrements**		
4. **unornamental**		
5. **cortége**		
6. **latent**		
7. **barouche**		
8. **crape**		
9. **equipage**		
10. **subtle**		

Name: _____   Date: _____

Learning Station Four: Making Inferences

Directions: Examine Document E, photograph of Abraham Lincoln. Begin by looking at the photograph as a whole; then focus on his facial features. Record your observations in the graphic organizer. Then read Document D, Walt Whitman's journal entry for August 12, 1863. Answer the question.

Detail (What I Observe)	This leads me to question...	Inference (My Best Guess)

Compare your observations of the photograph with Whitman's description of Lincoln in his journal entry for August 12, 1863. Cite textual evidence to support your answer.

_____

_____

_____

_____

_____

_____

Name: _____ Date: _____

Reflection

American Civil War: Characteristics of a Leader

Directions: Abraham Lincoln was the sixteenth president of the United States. His experiences in life helped to develop his personality and character. Reflect upon what you have learned about Abraham Lincoln from the primary and secondary sources. Examine the "Personality and Character Traits" handout. Select three traits that you feel Abraham Lincoln possessed that made him an effective leader. Cite textual evidence from the primary and secondary sources to support your choice of character traits.

_____

_____

_____

_____

_____

_____

_____

_____

_____

_____

_____

_____

_____

_____

_____

_____

_____

_____

_____

_____

_____

_____

Personality and Character Traits

adaptable	determined	immature	proud
adventurous	discouraged	impatient	rash
affectionate	dishonest	impulsive	reliable
aggressive	disrespectful	incompetent	reserved
ambitious	dreamer	indecisive	respectful
angry	eager	independent	responsible
anxious	easy-going	insecure	romantic
annoyed	eloquent	intelligent	rude
apologetic	embarrassing	inventive	ruthless
argumentative	encouraging	irritable	sarcastic
arrogant	energetic	jealous	scared
awkward	expert	jovial	secretive
boring	faithful	lazy	self-centered
bossy	fearless	leader	selfish
brave	fidgety	light-hearted	sensitive
calm	fierce	logical	serious
capable	flamboyant	lonely	shrewd
careless	flexible	lovable	shy
cautious	foolish	loyal	silly
charming	friendly	malicious	sly
cheerful	frustrated	mean	smart
clever	funny	meek	sneaky
cold-hearted	furious	mischievous	spoiled
compassionate	generous	mysterious	squeamish
compulsive	gentle	nagging	stingy
conceited	giving	naïve	strong
concerned	glamorous	nervous	stubborn
confident	gloomy	obedient	studious
confused	gracious	obnoxious	successful
considerate	greedy	observant	sympathetic
consistent	grouchy	optimistic	talented
controlling	gullible	patient	thankful
cooperative	happy	patriotic	thoughtful
courageous	hard-working	perceptive	thrifty
cowardly	hateful	persevering	timid
crafty	helpful	persistent	trusting
creative	hesitant	persuasive	trustworthy
cruel	honest	picky	unfriendly
curious	hopeful	polite	unhappy
demanding	hospitable	popular	wise
dependable	humble	practical	witty

Answer Keys

Instructional Resources
Recognizing Fact and Opinion (p.6)
1. F   2. F   3. O   4. F   5. O
6. F   7. O   8. O   9. O   10. F
11. F   12. F   13. F   14. O   15. O

Document-Based Learning Activities
Single Source
Exercising My First Amendment Freedoms (p. 8)
Rights (in any order): freedom of religion, freedom of speech, freedom of the press, freedom to peaceably assemble, freedom to petition the government for redress of grievances
Answers will vary for how students exercise those rights.

William Clark's Journal Entry (p. 9)
Answers may vary (example shown).
April 1, 1805

    We have thunder, lightning, hail, and rain today. It is the first rain of note since October 15th. I had the boat, pirogues, and canoes put in the water. We expect to set off the boat with dispatches. In the boat will go 6 Americans, 3 Frenchmen, and perhaps several Arikara chiefs. Immediately after, we shall ascend in 2 pirogues and 6 canoes accompanied by 5 Frenchmen who intend to ascend a short distance to trap beaver. The beaver is in great abundance. Higher up our party will consist of one interpreter and hunter, one Frenchman as an interpreter and his two wives (This man speaks Minitari to his wives who are Shoshone or Snake Indians of the nations through which we shall pass, and to act as interpreters through him.), 26 Americans and French, my servant, a Mandan Indian, and provisions for 4 months.

Clothing for Prairie Travelers (p. 12)
1. health and comfort
2. Cotton or linen fabrics do not sufficiently protect the body against the direct rays of the sun at midday, nor against rains or sudden changes of temperature. Wool, being a non-conductor, is the best material for this mode of locomotion, and should always be adopted for the plains.
3. Deep snow footwear: moccasins are preferable to boots or shoes, as being more pliable, and allowing a freer circulation of the blood.
   Summer footwear: shoes are lighter, and do not cramp the ankles; the soles should be broad, so as to allow a square, firm tread, without distorting or pinching the feet.
4. The awl and buckskins were necessary for repairing worn out shoes. Without shoes the feet could become damaged and the men would be disabled.

With no way to transport a disabled man, the solution was to prevent them from becoming disabled by being able to repair the shoes.
5. Possible answers: pants, moccasins

The President Makes a Proclamation (p. 15–16)
1. Abraham Lincoln issued the Emancipation Proclamation. The document states after the title "By the President of the United States of America." The proclamation is signed by Abraham Lincoln.
2. The purpose of the Emancipation Proclamation was to free any persons held as slaves within designated states. The proclamation declared "all persons held as slaves within any state or designated part of a State, The people where of shall then be in rebellion against the United States, shall be then, thenceforward, and forever free."
3. The proclamation gave the military and naval authorities the power to maintain the freedom of the freed slaves. The proclamation states "The Executive government of the United States, including the military and naval authorities thereof, will recognize and maintain the freedom of said persons."
4. Abraham Lincoln stated his authority for issuing the proclamation as "President of the United States" and as "Commander-in-Chief, of the Army and Navy of the United States."
5. Lincoln encouraged the freed slaves to "abstain from all violence" and "labor faithful for reasonable wages."
6. Yes, slaves were allowed to join the military. The proclamation stated "persons of suitable condition, will be received into the armed service of the United States."
7. Lincoln stated the proclamation was "warranted by the Constitution, upon military necessity."

A Letter of Consolation (p. 18)
1. Executive Mansion, in Washington on November 21, 1864.
2. Boston, Mass.
3. five sons. Lincoln stated "you are the mother of five sons."
4. It was the Civil War. The letter is dated November 21, 1864. The date of the Civil War was 1861–1865.
5. Lincoln's purpose for writing the letter to Mrs. Bixby was to console and thank Mrs. Bixby on behalf of the nation for her sacrifice. He stated "but I cannot refrain from tendering (to) you the consolation that may be found in the thanks for the republic they died to save."
6. Lincoln described his words as "weak and fruitless."
7. Lincoln hoped she would be left with "the cherished memory of the loved and lost" and "solemn pride."

Word Meaning (p. 20)

1. yellow
2. bountiful
3. a way or access road
4. verify
5. white

Interpreting a Poem (p. 21)

1. to express her feelings about America
2. The tone is positive. Positive words and phrases such as "O Beautiful," "patriot dream," "brotherhood," "self-control," and "freedom" were used.
3. In the first stanza, the poet uses phrases such as "spacious skies," "purple mountain majesties," and "fruited plains" to describe the beauty of all the different geographical scenery of the nation.
4. The author calls on God in each stanza: "God shed His grace on thee," "God mend thine ev'ry flaw," and "may God thy gold refine."

Analyzing a Photograph (p. 23)

Answers will vary, but may include:

1. ten-years-old; dirty and rumpled clothing; wears a hat with lint clinging to it; serious facial expression with mouth set in a grimace
2. taking off an empty thread bobbin and replacing it with a full bobbin
3. It was a period in history where children worked in factories. Conditions in the factory were not clean or safe.

To the Soldiers of the National Army (p. 25)

1. Soldiers of the National Army
2. Remind the soldiers that their actions would be "watched with the deepest interest" by their loved ones, "the nation," and "the eyes of all the world" and to keep themselves "fit and straight" and "pure and clean."
3. to "add a new laurel to the crown of America"
4. He said "this great war draws us all closer together, makes us all comrades and brothers, as all true Americans felt themselves to be when we first made good our national independence."

Help America Win! (p. 27)

1. construction workers who were building the warships
2. The building of ships was "more than a construction job," it was a "chance to win the war." By doing their best, they were doing their fair share like a soldier, a "man who fights."
3. The purpose of the poster was to encourage workers to do their "best."
4. It encouraged the workers to do their best work or they would not be helping their "son, brother, or pal who was 'OVER THERE.'"

Multi-Text Sources
The Birth of Freedom (p. 32)

1. Answers will vary but might include:
   Introduction – purpose of the resolution
   Rights – explains basic human rights all people have
   Grievances – list of complaints against the King of England
   Conclusion – Declaration of Independence and pledge by the signers
2. Adams felt the passing of the resolution was of great importance. He stated in his letter "the greatest question was decided, which ever was debated in America."
3. Adam stated the Declaration would give the "causes which have impelled us to this mighty revolution," and would state the reasons "which will justify it in the sight of God and man."
4. Adams had mixed feelings. He stated in his letter he was aware of the cost "the toil, and blood, and treasure, that it will cost." Yet he could see "the rays of ravishing light and glory" in the end.
5. the people of the United States can assume the "separate and equal station to which the Laws of Nature and of Nature's God entitle them"
6. Answers will vary. (See: Document A: The Declaration of Independence handout.)
7. The signers of the Declaration pledged "our Lives, our Fortunes, and our sacred Honour."

Dear Mrs. Roosevelt (p. 35)

Answers will vary.

Japanese-American Relocation and Internment (p. 38)

1. "every possible protection against espionage and against sabotage to national-defense material, national-defense premises, and national-defense utilities"
2. Secretary of War and Military Commanders he might appoint from time to time
3. The Secretary of War or the Commanders had the right to set up "military areas wherever they deemed it necessary. They could also "determine, from which any or all persons may be excluded, and with respect to which, the right of any person to enter, remain in, or leave shall be subject to whatever restrictions the Secretary of War or the appropriate Military Commanders may impose in his discretion."
4. By not listing ethnic groups, they could apply the executive order to whomever they wanted to. This way, their ability to carry out the executive order was not limited.
5. (1) openly admit that the government's actions were wrong
   (2) to apologize

(3) provide a public education fund to prevent similar actions from reoccurring

(4) make restitution (make good financially or restore honor) to the Japanese who were interned or their descendants

(5) discourage future violations and actions

(6) make U.S. complaints about human rights violations by other nations more credible and sincere

6. individuals with Japanese ancestry
7. relocation and internment
8. "racial prejudice, wartime hysteria, and a failure of political leadership"
9. The executive order was issued by the President of the United States. It established military areas and ordered the relocation and internment of people for the purpose of national defense during wartime. The public law was enacted by Congress to apologize, make restitution, and take steps to discourage such actions from happening again.
10. In 1942, the U.S. was at war with Japan. When the executive order was issued, they felt they needed to do this to protect the nation against espionage. In 1988, documentation by the commission proved the actions were "carried out without adequate security reasons and without any acts of espionage or sabotage."

Text With Audio/Visual Sources
Dust Bowl Days (p. 43)
Answers will vary, but may include:
1. erosion, high mounds of dirt, bare trees, buildings look abandoned (no evidence that people are living there), no crops in the field, dirt mound is rippled like the sands of the desert
2. There were no crops in the field, because the "crops failed." The buildings looked abandoned because "farmers couldn't make mortgage payments on their farms" so "thousands of families migrated west." It was sand that "settled around homes, fences, and barns."

War Is Declared! (p.46)
1. speech/address
2. December 8, 1941
3. Franklin D. Roosevelt
4. Congress of the United States and the people of the United States
5. declare a state of war with Japan
6. The document is creditable because it was a speech given by the President of the United States at the time of the historical event.
7. The central theme of the document is the justification for declaring war on Japan. In his speech President Roosevelt states "Yesterday, December 7, 1941... the

United States of America was suddenly and deliberately attacked by naval and air forces of the Empire of Japan."
8. Answers will vary.
9. Answers will vary.

Learning Stations Activity
Learning Station One: Compare and Contrast (p. 54)
Answers will vary.

Learning Station Two: Bias and Point of View (p. 55)
1. He thought his brother was "utterly foolish" for trying to sell the land and move to Missouri.
2. Answers will vary but might include: Lincoln argued if the land was sold, his brother would spend half his money "in moving to Missouri" and the other half he would "eat, drink, and wear out." Then he would have no money to buy land, not even "a spot big enough to bury you in."
3. Answers may include: anxious; foolish; it is my duty; foolery; idled; pretences; deceive; nonsense.
4. Answers will vary.

Learning Station Three: Word Meaning (p. 56)
Dictionary Definitions:
1. lodging or residence
2. cavalry sword
3. items a soldier wears other than his clothing or military equipment
4. not showy
5. ceremonial procession
6. underlying
7. a type of horse-drawn carriage
8. a gauze-like type of fabric
9. carriage and horses
10. restrained

Learning Station Four: Making Inferences (p. 57)
Answers will vary.

Reflection (p. 58)
Answers will vary